Relationships

Not long ago I walked by a wall poster that brought me back for a second look. I can't remember the artwork, but I've never forgotten the pithy, pointed message:

"Involvement with people is always a very delicate thing . . . It requires real maturity to become involved and not get all messed up."

How true! And yet there is nothing more important than involvement with other people. In point of fact, I cannot be rightly related to God without being rightly related to other people. The very test of my relationship with God is my relationship with other people. "By this shall all men know that you are my disciples, that you love one another." But how do you do it and not "get all messed up"? How do you make relationships in the first place?

Often we stumble along not knowing what is wrong in our relationships or how they could be developed or improved. We believe they were meant to be more satisfying, but we don't know the steps to that goal. This booklet offers some guidelines to be considered, some traps to be avoided, some directions to be followed.

I would like to suggest a very simple "ABC" concept that has proven to be very effective in understanding the nature of relationships. It is so helpful because you can apply it no matter where you are in life—no matter what relationships you are involved in, whether you're married or single, dealing with a same-sex or opposite-sex relationship.

Relationships: Why Bother?

Before we consider this "ABC" concept, let's consider why in the world we bother with relationships anyway. God gives us two basic reasons in His statement regarding Adam. Although at this point He is talking about man and wife, He gives us the basic principles or purposes for any kind of relationship. The Lord said, "It is not good for the man to be alone. I will make a helper suitable—or corresponding—to him" (Genesis 2:18).

The two purposes for relationship, then, are first: *"It's not good to be alone"*—in other words, we need relationships to prevent isolation.

Second, *we need "a helper"*—someone suitable to provide assistance to do God's will. When God said this about Adam and Eve, Adam didn't need a helper to put dinner on the table. They picked it off the trees. He didn't need a helper to mend his clothes. He didn't wear any. He didn't even need any help washing dishes. What then was Eve to do? She was to help him do the will of God, exercising dominion over the earth and populating it.

Why is isolation "not good"? The joy of companionship is the obvious reason; but there's a deeper one. We do not grow far spiritually in isolation. It is comparatively easy to relate to God when we are alone. I am never more godly—more pure, holy, upright—than when I'm all by myself . . . when I am out in the mountains on an exhilarating hike, or watching a sunset across a quiet lake. If I'm totally alone, God and I have marvelous times. And I think I can grow without other people. Just God and me. Everything is fine until I meet somebody who annoys me or frustrates me or angers me. Suddenly, all the warm fellowship I was so enjoying in my quiet time is put to the test.

The other morning I was studying the section of Proverbs that says, "A fool shows his annoyance at once, but a prudent man overlooks an insult" (Proverbs 12:16). I said to the Lord, "You know, that's great, that's tremendous! That's where I want to be, Lord. That's for me today." Within two hours after I arrived at my office, I *did not* ignore what I saw as an insult. I showed my annoyance immediately! All of the good spiritual input that we receive and enjoy is put to the test as we relate to other people. My real growth that morning did not take place as I was reading the Bible verse and thinking, "Isn't that marvelous?" The real growth came from blowing it and realizing I had really blown it. "Lord, forgive me. Wrong way. No good. Bring me another test and help me respond properly." That is growth.

We need other people—relationships. We need people to expose to us where we fall short of doing the will of God. We also need them to encourage us, challenge us, and hold us accountable. Scripture affirms this again and again.

Proverbs has an important statement regarding isolation. "An unfriendly man pursues selfish ends, and he defies all sound judgment" (Proverbs 18:1). An unfriendly man is a selfish man. He is one who is absorbed in his own interests. The isolated person is an individualist. "I can do it all myself. As long as my life is right with God, everything is okay. I can do without people. In fact, people get in the way of my goals." That sort of attitude leads to competition, grasping, and self-centeredness. This is the opposite of the helper role with its attitude of cooperation, giving, and other-centeredness.

The ABCs of Relationships

What then are relationships all about? What kinds are there? How can we make good ones and avoid pitfalls. Let's consider these questions under the ABC concept of Figure 1.

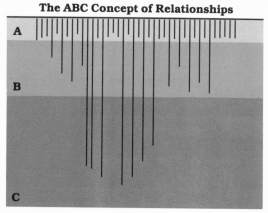

The ABC Concept of Relationships

A

B

C

Figure 1

The baseline represents no relationship whatsoever. The short lines indicate those with whom I have a little depth of relationship. That's the A level, the "Acquaintance" level. I know these people by name, and perhaps what they do, and that's just about all I know. I know *who* they are.

The B level you can call the "Brotherly" level. At the Brotherly level I not only know *who* they are, but *what* they're about: what their interests are, what they enjoy doing, what they don't enjoy doing, what they plan to do in the future, where they've been in the past. I know not only *who*, but *what*.

The C level of relationship is the "Close" friend relationship. Here I know *why* they are and *where* they are. I really know them in depth.

What is the difference between the A level and the B level? At the A level my knowledge of the person is only vague. At the B level we do things together, have fun together, maybe work together, talk about interests together. I know their likes and dislikes. I ask them for help occasionally, and they ask me, but there isn't much commitment or much deep, intimate sharing.

Friendships at "C-Level"

When you come down to the C level, you come to a relationship of commitment and intimate sharing. What are the ingredients of a C level friendship? First of all, you take mutual responsibility to keep the relationship on track and growing.

C level relationships demand a variety of shared interests. That certainly does not mean that every interest has to be the same. *Some* variety is desirable. Nevertheless, the relationship needs a solid base of mutual interests.

At the C level you have values that are very much the same. Like values means there is agreement and compatibility rather than frustration and opposition over such things as the use of time and money, the choice of activities and lifestyle. That is one reason why marriage between one who personally knows the Lord and one who does not has built-in problems. Their value systems are quite different.

Common goals are another aspect of C level friendships. It is very difficult to have intimacy if your goals are very different. If you're not going in the same direction, the depth simply isn't going to be there.

As an individual, you need to be a person who has interests, one who has established values, who has goals in life. Without these you have little to share. Don't expect a relationship to develop just because you are alive and human. Friendships don't exist in a vacuum. They grow out of the turf of our shared enjoyments, convictions, and accomplishments.

Mutual attraction is also involved—just plain *liking* the other person, being really attracted to him/her. There are things about the other that just simply appeal—her sense of humor or his quietness, her warmth or sincerity. In other words, you respond emotionally to this person. Without mutual attraction, there is no momentum towards depth.

Mutual enjoyment is still another element of the close-friend relationship. You enjoy the same kinds of things and the other person's form of humor doesn't embarrass you.

C level relationships are not going to develop unless we take the time and effort to really know the other person in depth. It takes time to discover a person's true values—not simply those to which they give mental assent. It takes effort to discover another's aims in life and what is behind their lifestyle. We need to discover whether we have basic alikeness in these areas without which there will not be the "oneness" needed for a deep C relationship.

The most important thing our heart wants to know about friends is, can we trust them? Can we trust them with our secrets, or do they break confidences? Can we trust them with our weaknesses and failures, our hopes and our dreams, or will they at some point use what we have shared against us? How we long for friends we can really trust!

There is still something more needed for a close-friend relationship. It is the most important of all. That "something" is commitment. Such a rare quality these days! We want the pleasures of deep relationships but not the responsibilities. Recently I noticed a difference in the commitment level in such a small thing as the way I sign personal letters. Mine end with a simple: "Love, Pam." My grandmother Pamela, however, who was born in 1844, signed her letters: "Your devoted friend, Mela." "Love" is an expression of warmth and feeling (but with no strings attached). "Devoted friend" adds that commitment of will.

Commitment involves sticking by when my

friend is preoccupied, is in difficulty, or has failed. It means hanging in there when we are not getting what we want out of a relationship. It means staying with it when the well of spontaneous affection seems nearly dry. It is a commitment to my friend's highest good—regardless of personal cost.

How Can We Make Good Relationships?

Good relationships take good people and good structure. Let's consider the "people" part first. What does it take to be a friend? Cultivating a relationship involves knowing a person, developing trust, and loving.

Know Your Friends

Before someone else can come to know me—really know me—I need to learn how to share myself intimately and appropriately. I don't share with everyone; only those with whom I have a continuing relationship. I share at about the same level of self-disclosure as my friend is sharing. I move into intimate sharing slowly, by letting my friend know what I am thinking and feeling. I share my convictions and tell my joys and disappointments. I let her know my dreams. I share my weaknesses, failures, and fears as well as my victories and successes. I let myself be known. Without self-disclosure I can have numbers of casual friends, but no intimate ones. If I am going to have the help, support, encouragement, and reproof I need from my friend, I must be open with her. Another great benefit of openness is that as she accepts me just as I am, really knowing me, I experience the kind of unconditional love God has for me.

For me to know another person I need to be able to *listen* to that person. Whole-heartedly. Carefully. Intensely. And after I've listened I need to respond. Too often, however, the scenario reads something like this: My friend has something on her mind, something that's come up that's extremely important to her. She comes to me and tells me all about it. I listen to her, but as soon as she finishes I start on something about myself. I have listened (maybe my mind was on what she was saying, maybe it wasn't . . . let's give me the benefit of the doubt that I was really listening to her), but there was no responding.

When you're listening to a friend, you keep hearing her. You follow the conversation. You get into what she is talking about. You ask appropriate questions. And you let her keep on talking until she has thoroughly talked the subject through. Now you not only have responded to the content of what she said, but also to her emotions—her anger, her joy, her sorrow.

Sometimes we fool ourselves into thinking that we listen when we allow another to speak. I keep quiet for two minutes while he talks and then I get my turn. Sometimes I can hardly wait for the other person to finish so I can get my turn. But that isn't listening. And it certainly isn't responding to what the other person has said, to what he hasn't said, or to where he's really coming from. It isn't becoming involved with him mentally and emotionally.

If I am going to develop and maintain a good friendship, I have to be able both to reveal who I am and to listen to the other person. Usually we are stronger in one area than the other. One will come more naturally. It will take real work to correct the weakness.

Another area that requires hard work is that of confrontational skills. When I disagree with a friend, which of the three ways of solving that disagreement do I use? Do I *strike out, walk out,* or *talk out*? Striking out can be done directly with angry words or obliquely with sarcasm. Walking out can be physically leaving or emotionally withdrawing or clamming up. Many of us know of no other way of handling conflict than these two. Talking out is foreign to us, and requires much concentration and practice. Striking out and walking out can shatter relationships, destroying any potential for growth.

Be Trustworthy

Being a good friend demands that I be someone my friend can trust. It means I will be loyal to my friend and keep confidences. I will be supportive of her in her interests, endeavors, heartaches. How much it means to have a supportive person alongside of you! How many marriages are hurting because of the lack of supportiveness!

The flip side of loyalty is that I will never betray my friend, nor will I desert him. Trustworthiness is a rare jewel. It is interesting to note that the first thing said about God's ideal woman in Proverbs 31 is "the heart of her husband trusts in her, and he will have no lack of gain. She does him good and not evil all the days of her life" (Proverbs 31:11-12 NAS).

What does it mean to do "good"? It means I will do all in my power to improve his life, to add to his sense of self worth, to help him develop his potential to the fullest. I am not here to compete but to help him do the work and will of God.

What does it mean not to do "evil"? It means I will defend him. I will not betray him. I will not talk behind his back, telling of his faults, injuring his reputation. I will not lie to him, break promises, use or hold against him what he has shared with me, nor undermine his self-confidence by continual criticism.

I will not desert him. And this means so much more than leaving physically. It also means I will not withdraw my acceptance of him. I will not make that acceptance conditional upon his complying with me or cooperating with me or conforming to my standards. It means I will neither withdraw my interest nor my care. Temptations to desert may arise when others come along who seem to have "more to offer." Loyalty means I will steadfastly refuse that option.

When a spouse or a friend knows that I will do him good and not evil and that I will continue on that course all the days of my life, his heart can trust, can be safe and at rest in me.

"All the days of my life" speaks of the commitment of a close friend. My grandmother once said to me, "A close friend is the most valuable possession you will ever have—and the most costly." Commitment costs. There is much giving, much self-sacrifice involved. These are not popular words in our day. Nor easy in any day. If, however, I want to develop and maintain deep, close friendships, this is the path I must be willing to follow.

Be Loving

Relationships involve not only knowing another and developing trust, but the emotional component of loving. Our hearts as well as our heads must be satisfied. What must be true of me in this aspect if I am to be a good friend? Warmth toward my friend is essential. That warmth needs to be consistent, not warm one day and cool the next. Personal warmth is the most powerful way we have of saying "I like you." It is the strongest factor in making and maintaining relationships. I need to be sure I am conveying that warmth to my friend, letting him know that I like him, approve him, and accept him as he is. *Affection needs to be verbalized.* Too often after relationships have developed, we settle into a satisfied silence, taking for granted the other person knows how we feel. But we all need continual reassurance.

Work Hard!

Finally, to be a good friend I need to make sure that I'm doing my part to maintain the relationship. When one person is working hard at this and the other isn't . . . well, it gets very old after a while. The person who has been putting in a lot begins to feel devalued. When we neglect to invest time and effort in a relationship, it telegraphs a signal to the other person which reads: "I really don't care that much."

Maintaining a continuing relationship will also require that I be a forgiving person. Since we are all fallen people—though we bear the image of God—I will have to forgive and be forgiven often. The Bible puts it directly: "Bear with each other and forgive whatever grievances you may have against one another. Forgive as the Lord forgave you. And over all these virtues put on love" (Colossians 3:13-14). This will involve bearing with weaknesses and idiosyncrasies. It means clearing up misunderstandings as soon as they arise. It means dealing with my pride and asking for forgiveness, dealing with my desire to punish and freely granting forgiveness.

Establish Structure in Your Relationships

Good relationships take both good people and *good structure.* But we don't like to hear that word "structure" in relation to friendships, do we? It grates on the ear a little. We feel friendships should be "spontaneous." Free. Relaxed. Yet lack of definition is precisely the reason why so many relationships break up. Every relationship that you are in right now, every relationship you will ever be in *will* be structured. If you don't play a part in establishing that structure, you may not like the framework that is set and you may want to get out of the relationship.

Structure the Limits

What things need to be structured? Structure the limits. How much time are you each going to be putting into this relationship? How much time can be counted on? I think of a neighbor of mine. The way our relationship is structured, she feels free to come over for about a half hour on Saturday mornings. I feel free to do the same thing. We don't expect to be spending three hours together on Saturday. This is the depth of our relationship.

What will be the limits of involvement? In

times of crisis, we must do what we can to help others—regardless of our level of friendship. But there are limits to involvement even then. The good Samaritan paid for but did not personally care for the wounded man at the inn. On a day-to-day basis, limits of involvement must be structured. Without such limits we are robbed of time and energy to meet our responsibilities to ourselves and others.

Structure the Responsibilities

What responsibilities will or won't you take on? When I go away for a few days or weeks my next door neighbor takes in my mail and waters my house plants. When she and her husband are away a few days or weeks, I feed their cat twice a day. These are responsibilities we are willing to assume. We do not, however, cut one another's lawns or water them.

What responsibilities can your friend expect you to assume? If you are asked to do something beyond what you would want to do or keep doing, then *say so*. Graciously, kindly, firmly. Yes it's difficult! But it is the kindest thing to do. It is foolish and counterproductive to accept an unwanted responsibility that will leave you with clenched teeth, upset stomach, and resentful spirit. That sort of "willingness" can only harm a relationship.

Structure the Expectations

What are the expectations? That needs some careful think-time. We often find ourselves uncomfortable with the structure of certain relationships, but we're reluctant to say anything, to declare what we are comfortable with. Too often, we promise "the world" as we enter into a relationship. "Any time you need me just say so." Taking me at my word my friend requests much more than I intended to give. I want to back out of it. I make some excuses. And then the other person really feels rejected. It's so easy to offer too much. We must establish realistic expectations from the beginning.

Structure the Roles

Roles in a relationship also need definition: who I will be to you, and who you will be to me. "No, I won't be your mother. No, I won't be your sister. No, I won't be your child. No, I won't be your best friend." It is vital to clarify roles early on. If you don't give any input, a role *will* be established for you. You may not like that role. You may be upset and feel trapped. As a result, the friendship you offer will be tentative and reluctant, leaving the other person hurt and confused. How much better to make it known right from the beginning what you will be. Then the other person knows where he stands. He has the opportunity to decide if he wants the kind of friendship you have to offer.

What Are the Problems That Can Develop in Relationships?

Too Deep, Too Soon

The most common problem in relationships is that of moving into depth too quickly. Proverbs 12:26 puts it well: "A righteous man is cautious in friendship." He moves slowly. He doesn't over-commit himself. Making friends slowly is basic to good relationships.

I remember as a kid I would sometimes run

home from school with big news for my grand-mother. "Oh Nanna! I have met the most wonderful little girl! We're going to be real pals. She just moved here and she's in my class, and oh, she's tremendous! We're going to be best friends." My grandmother would say to me, "Dear, you have to summer with her and winter with her, and summer with her again. Then tell me." There's great wisdom in that. It means you really get to know a person before entering into the commitments that a C level friendship requires.

Controlling the Other

The second most common problem is that of one person trying to control the other. The word *friend* comes from the Old English root word *frēon*—to love, akin to *frēo*—free. I must leave the other free, free to be herself. I must allow her to have her own feelings, think her own thoughts, do things her own way, make her own decisions. If I don't, she will feel she is being swallowed up and losing her own identity. Her alternatives are to either succumb to a destructive relationship or withdraw.

Competition

Competition is another blockbuster to relationships. God's purpose for relationships is mutual help through cooperation. But I want to be superior to my friend or spouse, so I compete. I want to look better or perform better or have more recognition. As a result, one or both of us has our sense of "being somebody" threatened and we respond by attacking or withdrawing. The relationship is strained or broken because somewhere along the line our objective shifted from "helping" to "winning."

Different Levels

Another common problem is that one person may want to be at one level, and another at a different level. The minute this situation occurs, you have conflict. The person at the deeper level tends to "put on the pressure." You feel yourself being pushed into a level of relationship you don't want. And that makes you resistant. You feel invaded, closed in on. You back up a level. That friend, you find, is always wanting to share, wanting your time, always wanting to move into your territory. Give him one hour and he wants two. Rather than opening up you find yourself looking for a back door.

What does this say to us, then? It says that you should never go any deeper in a relationship than the other person is ready to go. Proverbs 25:17 says, "Seldom put foot in your neighbor's house—too much of you, and he will hate you." Obviously, this verse is cautioning us not to overstay our welcome. But it is also saying this: Don't push too far into a friendship unless you're really wanted there. You will get resentment, not friendship, if you do.

If you find yourself at the C level and you sense that your friend wants only a B level, you have to back up to where he or she is. The more you try to pressure your friend into a deeper commitment, the more you're going to push him or her away from you. A number of years ago, I felt some very distinct relational pressure from a woman in my community. She was always giving me gifts.

After a number of weeks of this, I felt I was being bought. Obligated. And so I began to withdraw to an A level friendship. Really, I dreaded to see her come. Finally I had the courage to say to her, "Look, this is what's happening. I'd like to have a good friendship. It won't be as deep a friendship as you would like, but it could be a good friendship. There won't be intimate sharing, but we will be doing things together that we enjoy. Your gifts say to me that you want a close friendship. They make me feel obligated. Frankly the depth you want is not what I'm feeling I want right now. But I *would* like to have a friendship because I enjoy and appreciate you and want that to continue." She was furious at me. Well, I felt that was the end of that, but wished it hadn't ended that way. I tried to go on being kind, loving, and warm, but she was icy. Within about three weeks, however, she came back to me and said, "You know, you're the first person who's had the courage to tell me what's wrong in my friendships. I have never had a friendship of any depth. People have always backed away from me and I never really knew what was wrong." It hurt her to know what was wrong, and yet, because of that, she learned a vital truth about relationships. Since that time, she has gained—and kept—satisfying friendships.

Only One Friend

A third problem is having just one close friend. That can lead to poverty of personality at best, and exclusiveness at the worst. Great jealousies get into this kind of relationship. It is a most unhealthy pattern.

We should have friendships at all three levels. We should have many, many acquaintances. We need many B level friends. A variety of B level friends bring a lot of wealth into our personality. They have great treasures to give me, and hopefully I have some wealth to add to their lives as well. And then we need a number that are at the special C level. My growth as a person will come in large measure through my friends. To limit that number too far is to limit my personality.

Too Many Friends

On the other hand, not to draw any limits on the number of close friends poses another problem. We are finite beings, and we simply do not have the time or energy available to us to maintain more than six or seven really close friends.

If you examine the pattern of the Lord Jesus you will find He had many acquaintances. He had the crowds. He had His nine disciples at the B level. Then He had Peter, James, and John as close friends. Mary, Martha, Lazarus, and Mary Magdalene also were in that special group. Remember, He did not take all of His disciples to the Mount of Transfiguration. Only Peter, James, and John. He did not ask all of them to wait with Him at Gethsemane. Only those three. The Lord's pattern (as in the Chart) is an ideal we should be working towards. To try to take on too many close friends leaves them all disappointed and ourselves feeling harried, pressured, and often guilty that we can't respond to those we feel committed to. We need to be as free as Christ was to draw limits.

The Spouse As the Only Friend

The Lord's pattern is just as necessary for the married individual as for the single. We have placed such emphasis on the need for good, warm communication and great intimacy between husband and wife that we have made it sound as if this is the only relationship needed. No spouse can *possibly* meet all the emotional needs of the other for understanding and intimacy. We can drive one another away with excessive expectations and demands. Too heavy a burden is placed on the marriage. The marriage will be much richer and healthier if the spouses separately and together have many other relationships at varying levels, bearing in mind that C level relationships are reserved for our spouse and members of our own sex.

Break-up of Dating Relationships

Having worked with college and post-college age couples for twenty-six years, I've developed some deep convictions about dating relationships. If such a couple has been in a close relationship for a period of time, and for some reason one decides to break off the relationship, how should it be handled? I am convinced there needs to be a clean, sharp break. The tendency is to take one step back to a B level so as "not to hurt" the other person. A sensitive approach, but it does not work. If one person is still at C level, you cannot go back to B because the person whose heart is still involved will keep trying to pull the other back to a deeper level. For the sake of the person who is hurting, who is still emotionally involved, the relationship must be terminated. Until there is finality his hopes, dreams, and expectations are kept alive. All the old responses are still there. Emotions are kept raw and can still be hurting a year or two later. There is no gradual, step-by-step way to back out. A clean break is the most loving thing to do and represents a commitment to the friend's highest good. Why? Because it gives that person time to heal, so that eventually he or she can enter into deep involvement with another person. When both parties are happily involved with other committed C level dating relationships, then it is possible for the original couple to have a B relationship, but not before.

Undeclared Intentions

There is a very real need to keep declaring where you are in a dating relationship. It is so confusing to a fellow or girl not to know where the other sees the relationship. Let us assume, for example, that a fellow has been dating a girl for three or four months, and she doesn't know whether he is just enjoying a good friendship or is possibly working toward a lifetime commitment. It is most important for this man to declare where he is. He may say, "You know, I am just thinking of a friendship. I am not thinking of a serious, ongoing depth of relationship." Or, he may say, "You know, I really wonder whether or not this could be leading toward a very deep friendship and on to marriage."

College or post-college age fellows and girls cannot maintain a C relationship unless it is heading toward marriage. To tell themselves anything else is foolishness. Eventually, one is going to get hurt—perhaps profoundly. God made us sexual beings with sexual attraction. Deep intimacy of sharing between sexes arouses emotions and eventually desires for sexual fulfilment. That is the way God designed us. To try to maintain a C relationship with the opposite sex without an erotic component is going against nature. It is like telling the crocuses not to blossom in spring. This also holds true for married men and women in the office or any situation where deep sharing is entered into.

Mis-declared Intentions

Another problem arises when one says he or she is at a B level but acts as a person would at C. That needs to be refused. If you say, "We're just friends, this is not really heading to a lifetime commitment," then you don't share intimately, you don't reveal your secrets to the other. B level friends spend *maybe* one hour a week together. To indicate you would like to date a lot, that you would like to see the other many hours a week, and then to say there's really nothing in it is a mixed message. The one receiving it needs to say, "We are friends, therefore we'll do the activities, we'll have the discussions that mild friends have and see each other very occasionally." Otherwise one party can selfishly enjoy all the good of a relationship without the accompanying commitment, and that cheats the other.

Commitment Is the Bond

A woman to woman or man to man relationship, if it's going to be a very deep relationship, also requires a commitment. Commitment is the bond that holds relationships together through thick and thin. There are going to be times when your friend isn't free to do what you want to do. Friends may marry before you do, and naturally get involved in time and energy with their new family. They may not have very much time for you. What do you do then? Drop them? Not if you have a commitment. You weather through that time. Friends may be preoccupied with new interests or with heavy problems. They may not be functioning well physically or able to give emotionally. You don't drop them. "A friend loves at all times, and a brother is born for adversity" (Proverbs 17:17). You are not in the friendship, after all, only for what you can get out of it—you are in it to give, to bless. There are seasons in every relationship where one is called on to contribute heavily on the giving end. There may be years with a difficult elderly parent or a life-time with an indifferent spouse. Here is where commitment is tested, and here is where you will encounter God's greatest blessings.

The Ultimate Commitment

Commitment is the Lord's principle. What does He say about the way friendships should operate? "Lay down your life for your friends." He laid down His life for those who deserted Him in the garden and betrayed Him in the palace. He laid down His life for the non-loyal. And it is this laid-down life, He tells us, that leads us along the way of joy and fruitfulness. When in self-interest I ask, "What's in this for me?" He would restore me to His purpose for relationships and have me ask, "What can I give?"

Meanwhile, I have a Friend who never

changes. One who meets the deepest heart need. That is His commitment to me. But what of my commitment? Where would I place my relationship with Him on the ABC scale? How far am I involved in His interests? Are our values the same? Am I a trustworthy friend to Him, one who doesn't betray or desert? How much love do I express to Him? How deep is my commitment? If I want to deepen my relationship with the Lord Jesus, I need to approach it in the same way as with an earthly friend.

As for His commitment, He will never break His covenant, His vows to me. He is infinitely interested in all that concerns me. He thoroughly understands me, how I am put together, and where my strengths and weaknesses lie. He knows how I struggle against temptation. He understands my failures and victories. He loves me through and through with a love that is not "because" of anything in me. His very essence is love and His love toward me is uncaused and unconditional. Wonder of wonders, He, the God of the universe, has chosen to have a relationship with me. He is totally committed to me, committed every moment of every day to act for my highest good. And best of all, He is committed to never betray me and never desert me "all of my days."